THE BEARS'
BOOK OF
COLORS

Jocelyn Wild

IDEALS CHILDREN'S BOOKS

Nashville, Tennessee

First published 1989 in the United States
by Ideals Publishing Corporation,
Nelson Place at Elm Hill Pike, Nashville, TN 37214

Copyright ©1989 Jocelyn Wild
Printed in Hong Kong

ISBN 0–8249–8296–7

One day three little bears went
to play in the meadow.

After a while a big cloud came
into the sky. It started to rain.
"I'm getting wet!" said Griff.
"So am I," said Snuff. "Let's run
for shelter under that big rock."
"Run!" shouted Pawpaw.
"It's POURING!"

All the bears ran to the rock
and stood underneath it.
It rained and rained.
"It's boring just standing here,"
said Griff.
"Let's play 'I spy'," said Snuff.
"I'll start. I spy something RED."

"There isn't anything red,"
said Pawpaw. "There's only
gray. Gray rock and gray rain."
"Yes, there *is* something red,"
said Snuff. "It's red, and it's very
small, and it's crawling up my paw."
"I can see it!" said Griff. "It's a …

RED LADYBUG

"It's my turn now. I spy something
BROWN."
"Easy," said Snuff. "Brown bears!"
"No," said Griff. "There's something
else. It's brown and it's wet. And
Mother Bear doesn't like it when
we get it all over us."
"I know!" said Pawpaw. "It's …

BROWN MUD

He looked very hard at the mud.
"I spy something PINK," he said.
"It's pink and long and slippery."
"Your tongue!" said Snuff.
"No," said Pawpaw. "Anyway,
I can't see my tongue."
All the bears stuck out their
tongues and tried to see them. But
it was difficult because their noses
got in the way. Then Griff noticed
something wriggling in the mud.
"I've got it!" he cried. "It's a ...

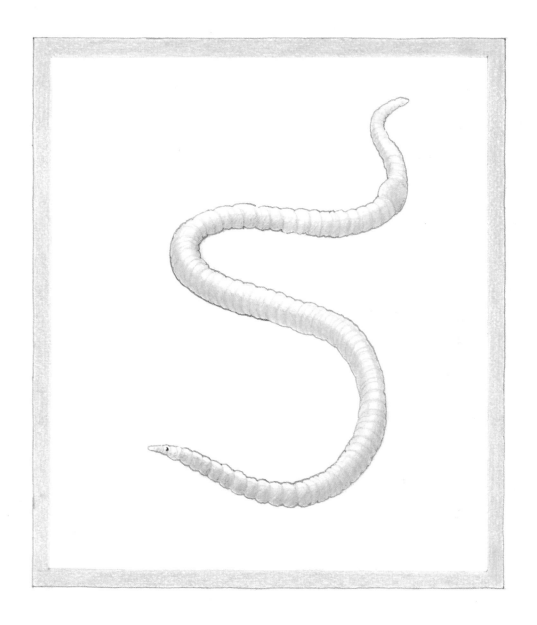

PINK WORM

"Now it's my turn," said Griff.
"I spy something YELLOW.
It's yellow, and there are lots
and lots and LOTS of them!"
"I see them!" said Snuff.
"They're ...

YELLOW
FLOWERS

"Now," said Snuff, "I spy something
GREEN."
"Leaves!" said Pawpaw.
"Grass!" said Griff.
"You nearly said it then," said Snuff.
"I know!" said Pawpaw. "It's a …

GREEN
GRASSHOPPER

"Now it's my turn. I spy something
BLACK. It's black, and it flies."
"A fly!" said Snuff.
"A bat!" said Griff.
"No," said Pawpaw. "It flies and
it says *Caw.*"
"You're cheating," said Snuff.
"You can't see any birds."
"I can't see any birds," said
Pawpaw, "but I can see a …

BLACK FEATHER

"Feathers don't say *Caw*!" said
Snuff and Griff both at once.
Pawpaw pretended not to hear them.
"My turn again," he said quickly.
"And I can see something ORANGE.
It's orange, and it flies."
"Not another feather!" said Snuff.
"I suppose it says *Caw* too?"
"No," said Pawpaw. "It doesn't
make any sound at all."
"I see it now!" said Griff. "It's an ...

ORANGE
BUTTERFLY

The bears tried to catch the
butterfly, but it flew away.
Suddenly Snuff said, "I spy something
WHITE. It's what bears like to eat!"
"Where?" cried Griff at once.
"What is it?" said Pawpaw.
"We give up!" they both said.
"Here it is," said Snuff. "It's a ...

WHITE
MUSHROOM

In fact it was three mushrooms.
Snuff picked the mushrooms, and
the bears ate them up.
"Hey!" said Griff, "I spy
something PURPLE!"
"It's not your turn," said Snuff.
"It's purple, and it's juicy, and I'm
going to eat it NOW!" said Griff.
"I'm going to eat one too," said
Pawpaw. "It's a …

PURPLE
BLACKBERRY

"Blackberries aren't purple," said
Snuff. "They're black! That's why
they're called 'black berries.'"
"Not when you eat them!" said Griff.
He stuck out his tongue. It was all
purple with blackberry juice.
For a while the bears were busy eating
blackberries. Then Snuff said,
"I spy something BLUE! It's blue,
and it's big, and it's so high
you can't touch it!"
"We can see it!" shouted Griff and
Pawpaw together. "It's the …

BLUE SKY

"And look! It's stopped raining!"
The three little bears ran out from
the rock. And suddenly they stopped.

"Look at that!" cried Griff.
"Isn't it pretty!" said Snuff.
"Oh look!" shouted Pawpaw, "It's a …

RAINBOW

LOOK AT ALL THE COLORS!

The End